The Chinese Puppet Theatre

The Chinese Puppet Theatre

SERGEI OBRAZTSOV

Translated from the Russian by

J. T. MacDermott

PLAYS, INC.
Publishers
Boston

First published in mcmlxi
by Faber and Faber Limited
24 *Russell Square London W.C.*1

Reprinted 1975

This book comprises a chapter, originally entitled *My Colleagues*, from *The Chinese Theatre*, published by The State 'Art' Publishing House, Moscow, 1957

ISBN O-8238-0194-2

Printed in the United States of America

Illustrations

(AT THE END OF THE BOOK)

I have been giving puppet performances for more than thirty years now and have been directing the State Central Puppet Theatre for a quarter of a century.

When members of our theatre audiences visit our 'puppet' museum, either before shows or during intervals, they find themselves being observed by puppets not only from the Soviet Union, but also from Italy, France, Britain, U.S.A., Germany, Czechoslovakia, Hungary, Poland, Rumania, India, Burma, Turkey and Persia. But until quite recently we have not had a single puppet on display from China, except for a few examples of shadow puppets.

Although our library shelves contain many books devoted to puppetry, apart from the Chinese 'shadows' there is nothing, or practically nothing, mentioned in any of the books in any language about the Chinese puppet theatre.

Prior to my visit to China, I did not therefore even suspect that the Chinese puppet theatre had developed so far, nor was I aware of its traditional character.

The first puppet performance I saw in Peking was, for me, an entirely new discovery, or, more correctly, a chain of new discoveries, for on that occasion I saw a number of short sketches, each of which was unexpected in both form and content.

The performance took place in a room under conditions which were unusual for this particular form of the Chinese puppet theatre, in so far as it was typical street theatre; it was very small from the point of view of the number of puppeteers involved—there was only one—while the playboard itself was minute. The whole thing is easily carried about on a 'beam' or 'yoke' which rests on the actor's shoulders, and is therefore referred to as a 'portable booth'. This beam also serves as a support for a charming little house with a covered terrace—the proscenium.

Naturally, a single vertical beam can only support the small house from below, but cannot prevent it from falling sideways, therefore the rear of the house is generally placed against a convenient fence, the wall of a peasant house or the village temple. A length of cloth is attached to the 'foundations' of the house, as it were, and reaches right down to the ground on three sides, thus concealing the puppeteer who stands under it.

Structurally, the 'portable booth' is not at all like my puppet stage, the arrangement of which I learned from the popular Russian puppeteer, Ivan Finogenovich Zaitsev. But in its mobility, its portableness and in the way it is carried round from place to place, i.e. in its function, it corresponds exactly, not only with the 'one man' theatres in which our Russian Petrushka used to perform, but also with booths used for similar performances by the French Polichinelle, the English Punch, the German Hanswurst, the Italian Punchinello and the Czech Kašparek. But while it is similar in function, the characters are of course different.

All these heroes of the European puppet theatre I have mentioned, are endowed with their own national traits of character and have their own, purely national, repertoire, but, at the same time, this jolly roisterous band of puppets speaking different tongues have a sort of common ancestor. Place them side by side, and they will look just like each other as only brothers can. If they are not blood brothers then they are at least cousins; each has a long nose, a mouth stretching from ear to ear, a hump on his back—possibly two—a buffoon's hat with a tassel or baubles, and carries a stick.

Some historians of the European puppet theatre consider that the ancestor of the puppet hero of the streets was an Italian, others that he was an ancient Roman, while some think, with perhaps more justification, that it was the Turkish 'Karagöz', or 'Black Eye', since Karagöz also has a hunched back.

In China however, I found nothing similar to our Petrushka, or to Punch and Punchinello, nor did I come across any kind of puppet theatre where the repertoire always centred round one and the same character.

Nevertheless, from the first moment of the performance in this 'portable theatre', I felt, much to my surprise, that there were indeed associations with the Russian Petrushka. In order to explain what these associations were, and what similarities and differences there were, I shall first of all describe the first two short scenes which were presented by the Peking puppeteer, Yuan Fen-ku, who inherited this traditional art from his father, his grandfather and great-grandfather.

We sat down in front of the small multi-coloured house which was leaning against a wall, and from below which hung a piece of dark grey material like a long freely flowing skirt. A man of about twenty, dressed in a simple blue jacket and trousers, opened a flap in the material and disappeared under the little house, the foundations of which were taller than himself.

In the professional language of Russian puppeteers, the upper lintel of the stage is called a 'border', and in this case the leading edge of the playboard served as the 'border'. Judging by the fact that the length of this border was about sixty centimetres and the depth of the whole house including the terrace about the same, I realized that apart from the actor who had gone underneath, there was no one else there, since it would have been impossible to accommodate two people in such a small, restricted space.

Since it is unthinkable to imagine a popular Russian Petrushka show without an organ grinder standing alongside, I began looking closely about me for a musician. But there was no one anywhere near the stage and I therefore assumed that there would be no musical accompaniment.

My reflections were suddenly interrupted by the sharp clanging of gongs, and judging by the sounds there were two, of different sizes.

These sounds in themselves were no surprise to me, because all popular entertainments in China begin with the sounding of gongs, but what did surprise me was that, in this case they were inside the booth and the actor who was operating the puppets was beating the gongs as well. So there was going to be music after all! And indeed, it could not be otherwise.

The reverberating sounds of the gongs faded and a voice was heard from behind the stage. A lady interpreter translated into my ear: 'Smarten yourself up and go and call your elder sister.' I did not realize who had said this and I quietly asked the interpreter, who replied in a whisper and with some surprise: 'The puppeteer, Yuan Fen-ku of course!' 'Yes, I know that, but what I'm not clear about is whether they are his words or the words of the hero who is about to come on stage.' The interpreter did not have time to reply, for just then two small figures appeared on the playboard, and a voice from behind stage said something in an authoritative tone. There was a whisper close to my ear: 'Sing and be merry.' The little puppets sang in a high falsetto. Obviously the interpreter was right; the voice was that of the puppeteer himself. One of the puppets disappeared through a doorway and immediately came back again carrying a china plate. While they continued singing, the puppets began throwing the plate to each other with considerable skill. Actually it was the puppeteer who was throwing the plate from one hand to the other, because the puppets fitted on his hands were constructed just like our Petrushka or the English Punch. English people define the structure of these puppets clearly by referring to them as 'glove puppets'. In fact such puppets have no bodies. All they have is a head, tiny hands and a costume shaped like a three-fingered glove. The actor's hand becomes the body as soon as he fits the puppet over it. The index finger forms the head and neck, while the thumb and middle finger are inserted into the empty sleeves to form the arms.

Naturally the little jugglers on the puppet stage were not throwing the plate about in the same way as humans would, but clutched it with both little hands in the way that puppets do, and with such astonishing rapidity and skill that we began to applaud. The voice from behind stage said: 'The comrades are applauding. Take a bow!' The jugglers bowed, but the voice began to reproach them, saying: 'Throwing a plate about—that's not so very funny yet!' You ought to put it on your head!' One juggler, or to be precise, a female juggler, who was evidently the elder sister, began placing the plate on her brother's head, while maintaining, like puppets the world over, a concentrated seriousness. The plate slipped off and the voice said: 'That's a very tricky thing to do. It's not so easy to balance a plate on the head.' And it is in fact very difficult, since the head in question is, after all, small—a puppet head and not a human head. But just the same, the plate was balanced magnificently. We laughed, but the voice was still not silent: 'You're not being funny enough yet. You'll have to think up something else.' And the little jugglers obediently tried to devise more and more new tricks. The 'elder sister' placed a stick on her partner's head, then, putting the plate on top of the stick, she twirled it round with such force and skill that it began to revolve just as quickly as it does when real itinerant jugglers demonstrate this traditional Chinese art, using long bamboo canes. We went on laughing and applauding but the voice of the actor asserted that as far as he was concerned, it was still not nearly funny enough.

The stick suddenly became longer and the plate rose twice as high. This, incidentally, is not practised by real jugglers; it can only be done by puppets.

The plate goes on twirling round while the little jugglers sing a jolly song called 'I've been to Shanghai'. Craning her neck, the 'Elder Sister' sees how high the twirling plate has risen and, either from fright or naughtiness, jumps up and strikes the top of it. The stick disappears almost entirely into the juggler's head and the unfortunate brother begins to wail: 'Take it out of my head.' The sister calmly replies: 'That's not so easy', and begins turning the helpless brother round and round on the stick, thereby disclosing that the stick, which seemed to be balanced on his head, in fact extended right through the whole of his body. After this amusing revelation by the puppeteer the scene came to a close, accompanied of course, by the clanging of gongs.

A new character—an old shepherd—then emerged from a rear door on the left of the playboard. He announces that there is a great tiger which lives up on a mountain, and immediately adds: 'But I'm not afraid of the tiger. I'm going to seek him out and kill him.' The tiger appears and lies down on the edge of the playboard. The shepherd evidently is not only boastful but stupid, because, after taking one look at the tiger, he says, 'Oh! it's a pussy cat!' and begins to tickle it. The voice of the puppeteer warns: 'Don't be a fool! Don't meddle with the tiger.' The shepherd goes on tickling the sleeping tiger and then runs away. The puppeteer cries, 'Where are you running off to? Are you afraid then?' The shepherd reappears with a spear in his hand. 'No. I'm not afraid.' He pokes the tiger straight in the nose with it and declares: 'The tiger's dead. I'll have to take its skin and sell it. It's very valuable.' The shepherd sings and dances for joy and then, just to make finally sure that the tiger is dead, he shouts at it 'Tiger! Tiger!' It does not answer or budge. 'It's obviously quite dead. Now we'll have a lot of meat.' The tiger then springs up, opens wide its enormous jaws, swallows the stupid boaster and lies down to sleep again.

There is a voice from behind the stage. (At this point I can now distinguish between the voice of the puppeteer himself and the voice of any one of his puppets.) This is the voice of a new puppet. It is calling to someone. The interpreter whispers to me in Russian, 'The old man. The old man.' On the stage there is the puppet figure of a woman. She stumbles against the sleeping tiger and takes fright, while the voice of the puppeteer says: 'The tiger's just eaten the old man.' The woman seizes the spear and with all her strength she kills the tiger and from out of its dead jaws she drags her husband—frightened but still alive. She scolds him roundly and orders him: 'Carry me home.' The old man takes her on his back and to the loud clanging of a gong they disappear through a door on the right.

Like the previous one, the sketch with the tiger was performed with puppets worn on the hand, i.e. with what English people, as I have already said, call 'glove puppets'; in Germany they are called 'hand püppen', while more often than not, we call them simply 'Petrushkas'.

What was there new for me in these two sketches, and what were the associations I mentioned before I started describing them?

There was indeed much which was new and unexpected. First of all, both sketches were completely different in genre. One was clearly a parody—not a malicious one, but simply an ironical parody on street comedians like the puppeteer himself. The second was an everyday satire on stupidity and conceit. The heroes were different and the sketches themselves could have been performed in any order, since one did not necessarily follow on the other. This is one way in which the performances of the Chinese popular puppet theatre are very different from the old popular performances by Petrushka, Polichinelle, Hanswurst and Punch. All of these used to appear in a whole number of connected satirical sketches, in which the central hero was always one and the same unreal, abstract character, in whom the characteristics of a number of heroes could be clearly observed; for example, the 'gypsy', the 'corporal' and the 'doctor' as played by the Russian Petrushka.

But if the dramatic construction of the plays performed by the popular glove puppets of China differs so sharply from those of the old Russian Petrushka and similar puppets of Western Europe, then what was the common link between them? Simply the construction of the puppets? Yes, of course, their construction in the first place, but it was precisely this similarity which made me think again about the origin of glove puppets. The basic heroes of the European puppet theatre have common origins, and these origins are not to be found on Chinese territory—I did not see any puppets with hunched backs or long noses there—but evidently the system of glove puppets itself came to Europe from China, although I do not know when, or whether it came via Russia, India, Iran or Turkey. Theatrical historians will no doubt find the answer to this, if they ever seriously examine the history of popular entertainment.

But how can I substantiate my hypothesis? By documentary evidence? Possibly. References to the existence in Europe of puppets worn on the hands do not go further back than two or three centuries. In China, however, the existence of 'bag' puppets as they are called there, can be documentarily attested for many centuries earlier. But perhaps a simple comparison of puppets is much more convincing. Proof of the primogeniture of the Chinese 'bag' puppets can be found, first of all, in the perfection of their anatomical development and the exactness of their proportions, which indicate a centuries-old stage usage and an unbroken traditional chain.

Although itinerant puppeteers in both Europe and China showed their puppets in streets and squares on market days and popular festivals, it does not of course mean that they performed before large audiences. On the contrary, the number of spectators was always small, generally about fifty, perhaps a hundred, but not more. To watch a puppet show from a distance is unthinkable and therefore the size of an audience was restricted to the number of people forming a tight semi-circle round the stage. After all, the most interesting part of it all is the physical handling of a puppet—the way it moves, and you cannot really see all this from a great distance. The Chinese therefore evolved and perfected the proportions of these glove puppets, thus enabling them to move with the maximum possible expressiveness. Such puppets can only be observed from a short distance. If you are standing ten or fifteen yards away, you will not derive much pleasure from a performance, but on the other hand, from a distance of three or five yards, these puppets are simply wonderful to watch. So that it should be clear to my readers, the majority of whom are probably not very well acquainted with the secrets of the puppet theatre, what the particular features of these hand puppets are, I would ask you to imagine a man standing with raised hand behind a stage which is slightly taller than himself. As it is impossible to keep one's arm fully outstretched for a long time, it is slightly bent at the elbow, so that the spectators standing in front of the stage can see the puppeteer's hand and about ten centimetres of his wrist. If he puts his index finger into the puppet's head, you then have the full height of the puppet as seen by the audience.

At first glance it would seem advisable to make the puppet's head as large as possible so that the features might be more visible from a distance. But this only appears so initially, since the larger the head, the smaller the body becomes in proportion, and if you are trying to preserve a human appearance, the puppet would have to be seen only from about the waist up, or perhaps even less.

There are other snags apart from this one. The arms of a glove puppet are, after all, the actor's thumb and middle finger, and in comparison with a large head they would appear to be ridiculously short. True, they could be lengthened by means of cardboard tubes, but, in the first place, they would as a result become lifeless, like sticks, and secondly, the puppet would seem to have no shoulders at all.

If the proportions are ignored, then the body appears to be too small in relation to the head and the puppet would look rather like a young frog.

But this is still only half the trouble. The most important thing is that, with a large head and a small body, the movements of the puppet do not appear to be at all expressive. After all, a pose or a gesture depend, not so much on the head, as on the body and arms.

Therefore, unlike many of the fairground glove puppets of Europe in the eighteenth and nineteenth centuries, with their large wooden heads and clumsy bodies, the Chinese 'bag' puppets are remarkably proportionate, mobile and expressive. The head of one of these puppets is no more than four or five centimetres in diameter. If you can picture such a tiny head on the tip of your index finger, you will see at once how the actor's wrist forms the body of the puppet. It can bend forward, backward or sideways. The puppeteer's fingers are not lengthened by tubes and therefore the movements of the puppet's arms are free and elastic.

The movements of the puppets I was watching seemed to me

to be so natural that at one point it even struck me that the tiny fingers had also started moving. After a time the hallucination was repeated. I began to watch even more closely and I realized that it was not a hallucination at all. The fingers were in fact moving. Their joints were evidently movable. If the hand was turned palm upwards, all the fingers were stretched out in the same way, but as soon as it was turned palm downwards, two or three fingers dropped under their own weight. The result was either an imperative gesture, usual in male roles, with the index finger outstretched, or a female gesture, no less characteristic, with the index finger and the little finger stretched out, while the middle and second fingers are bent.

Later on, after I became acquainted with the structure of a large number of Chinese puppets, I realized that not all of them have movable fingers, but only those playing in certain roles, requiring such gestures. The hands of the other puppets were more or less immovable, or so constructed that they could hold swords, spears or shields. I also discovered that despite the diminutive proportions of the heads of 'bag' puppets, some of them had movable mouths and eyes.

I am aware that some of my readers, who know something about the Soviet puppet theatre might ask: 'What were you so surprised about? Aren't there quite a few puppets with movable mouths and eyes in the theatre you direct!' That may be so, but after all, we have a vast team of specialists in our theatre—artists, modellers, sculptors and mechanics. Each new puppet is designed and made according to the role it has to play. But in China, all these wonderful creations—and we really ought to adopt some of them—are the products of a centuries-old tradition. The glove theatre must have been very widely diffused throughout China, and have existed for a very long period, for tradition to have evolved such a perfect form.

But are the similarities and differences between the street

puppet theatre of European countries and China restricted only to the technique of puppet construction? No! There is another aspect of the Chinese puppet theatre, connected with the method of dramatic presentation which struck me as remarkable.

In order to explain this very interesting peculiarity I shall have to retrace my steps a little.

You remember that, before the performance began, I was looking round for a musician, and I recalled the organ grinder who is always present at any performance by the Russian Petrushka. This was not just because I was expecting musical accompaniment, but rather because the Russian organ grinder plays a definite part in a Petrushka show—a splendid and indeed indispensable part. The Russian Petrushka, as many of you probably know, always spoke in a peculiar, but clearly non-human voice. This curious sounding voice was produced by the puppeteer, who placed a kind of small 'whistle' or 'schwazzle' in his mouth, which he pressed to the roof of his mouth with the back of the tongue, and spoke through the narrow aperture of the 'schwazzle'. The voice was loud and shrill, but the words were not always very understandable, so the organ grinder always cross-examined Petrushka, whose lines he repeated wholly or in part. A dialogue would develop, but apart from its purely auxiliary function of increasing the intelligibility of Petrushka's squeaky voice, this dialogue also had a dramatic function—a full and remarkably fascinating contact was established between Petrushka and the organ grinder. He would warn Petrushka of any danger, give him advice, scold him for indecorous behaviour or question him about his future intentions. He was a living link between the audience and Petrushka, since he was a representative of both sides; as a human being he could consider himself part of the audience, and as an actor he was professionally on the same level as Petrushka. When I was a child, I remember very vividly the profound reality of the relationship which existed between us children and the organ grinder and Petrushka who used to come into one of the courtyards in Moscow.

On seeing a Chinese puppet show for the first time, I was very astonished to find that despite the absence of a musician, there was nevertheless an intermediary between the puppets and the audience. In this case it was the puppeteer himself, but his functions were the same as those of the Russian organ grinder. If one bears in mind that Chinese puppeteers sometimes use a 'whistle' giving off the same shrill noise as our Petrushka, then the similarity becomes even greater. Moreover, it is also very interesting to note that the voice which is produced by using this 'whistle' is referred to by the Chinese as 'U-dyu-dyu', and it springs to mind that in the Ukraine, a puppet speaking in such a squeaky voice is called a 'Vanka Ru-tyu-tyu'. This is probably only a phonetic parallel, because in both cases the name is onomatopoeic and the original sound is the same.

The third sketch performed for us by Yuan Fen-ku was entitled *Chu Pa-chieh and the maiden*—a dramatic episode from *Journeys to the West.*

A monk was on his way to India accompanied—apart from Sun Wu-k'un—by two others, Sha Hsieh-shan and Chu Pa-chieh. In translation the name Chu Pa-chieh means 'the pig of eight prohibitions'. These prohibitions had been imposed on Chu Pa-chieh by the monk, and one of these was that he should keep away from women. Sun Wu-k'un, who has the power of turning himself into anything he pleases, decides to test the steadfastness of Chu Pa-chieh, and assumes the form of a beautiful young woman. Naturally Chu Pa-chieh is not slow to act and, placing the beauty on his back, he carries her off homewards. The journey is a long one and several times Chu Pa-chieh goes out through a door on the right of the playboard and re-emerges from a door on the left. But the further he walks, the heavier his burden grows. Towards the end of the journey, when the exhausted

Chu Pa-chieh is already staggering, it becomes clear that he is no longer carrying the beautiful young maiden on his back, but the King of the Monkeys—Sun Wu-k'un.

I found this episode from *Journeys to the West* very interesting but I was astonished first of all to note that it was performed not by glove puppets, but by so-called 'rod' puppets. The construction of these puppets differs from that of glove puppets, in so far as they are operated by three rods. The puppet's head is attached to the central rod, and the other two rods are joined to the elbows or wrists of the puppet's arms. The central rod is concealed by the costume, and the rods coming out from the arms are either not hidden at all, or else screened by the same costume if it is wide enough, or by a special sleeve covering or the folds of a cloak.

Puppets of similar construction were used for the first time in the Soviet Union in the 1920's, when the Efimovs performed a fragment from Shakespeare's *Macbeth*. I don't know who gave the name to these puppets, but they became known as 'Javanese' puppets, as it was thought they originated in the island of Java.

In 1939, the State Central Puppet Theatre performed *Aladdin's Wonderful Lamp*, using rod puppets. Since then these puppets have been developed and their form has changed somewhat from performance to performance, so much so that the technical construction of the puppets used in *2–0 for Us* or in *The Devil's Windmill* are no longer very like the original Efimov puppets.

Rod puppets have now spread to many theatres in the Soviet Union and abroad. Several theatres in Poland, Czechoslovakia and Hungary have begun to use them, and I recently received a letter from an English puppeteer in which he writes that he has decided to use these in his productions.

When talking about the genealogy of rod puppets, I referred to the 'Efimov' puppets and to 'Javanese' puppets. But in Peking, when I saw the sketch featuring Sun Wu-k'un and Chu

Pa-chieh, in which rod puppets were used, it became clear to me that one could not regard the island of Java as their only home.

Rod puppetry has become one of the main methods employed in the Chinese puppet theatre. In their external form, their construction and their repertoire, the tradition of centuries is perhaps evident to a greater degree than in that of glove puppets.

Chinese puppeteers manipulate these rod puppets with consummate skill. To this day I cannot understand how a puppeteer, whom I saw performing in the town of Sian, succeeded, without any assistance whatsoever, in lifting a pliable bamboo yoke with buckets dangling from it with the two hands of a puppet, and placing it on the narrow shoulders of another puppet, in such a way that it swung freely at every movement and never fell off.

But when I saw string puppets for the first time in Shanghai, I realized that this system too had been evolved by the popular traditions of the Chinese theatre to a considerably greater degree than the marionettes of Western Europe.

In order to explain this to those readers who are not very well acquainted with the puppet theatre, I shall first of all have to say something about how string puppets are made to move.

The actor does not stand below as is the case when performing with glove or rod puppets, but on the contrary, he stands above the puppet. In his hands he holds what is called a 'control'. This is either a simple arrangement of crossed sticks or some other kind of structure whose complexity depends both on the traditions of a particular country and on the functional peculiarities of a particular puppet. To this 'control', strings are attached, the other ends of which are connected to various parts of the puppet. Usually two strings are attached to the shoulders and it is on these the puppet hangs. Two others are attached to the temples. If these are pulled tight, the head is raised, if slackened the head bends; and if the strings are tightened and slackened alternately, then the head will bend first to one shoulder then to the other, or it will turn round. A separate string extends to the waist, so that it is possible, by tightening this string, while at the same time slackening the shoulder string, to make the puppet bow. A similar string is attached to the stomach so that it can bend in the opposite direction; and one to each wrist and knee. With European marionettes, these last two strings are normally connected to a crossbar on a vertical 'control'. By moving the crossbar the puppet can be made to move its legs and begin to walk or dance. It is true that there have been, and still are, marionettes in Europe operated by a fewer number of strings. The normal minimum number is about eight or ten for each puppet. If it is desirable or necessary that the number of possible movements a puppet has to make should be increased, the number of strings used must also be increased and these are joined to the thighs, the toes, heels, ankles, etc.

As far as Chinese puppets are concerned, the control of movement has been worked out and elaborated by tradition to a degree which I could never possibly have imagined. I have seen puppets operated by twenty, thirty and even forty strings, and I have seen them move their mouths, their eyes and their eyebrows. I have seen astonishingly expressive mimicry on puppet faces resulting from the movements of brow and chin, and finally I have seen literally living hands capable of grasping any object.

I did not believe my eyes when, in the first scene of a performance in Shanghai, a puppet, representing a woman working at a weaving loom, lifted up a work basket containing thread with her hand and put it down again.

In European marionette theatres a string is generally attached to any object which a puppet has to pick up; this passes through a fixture in the puppet's palm and then upwards to the puppeteer's control'. Normally, this string hangs loose and it is difficult to see it. But when the time comes to pick up a sword, a glass or an apple, the hand of the puppet reaches out for the object, the string tightens and the apple literally sticks to the hand. In order to replace it, the string has to be released. The apple falls but the string remains attached to it, and it still continues to pass through the puppet's hand, thus impeding its freedom of movement.

During the performance in Shanghai I did not notice any strings attached to the basket of thread. The puppet picked up the basket in just the same way as you or I would have done and put it back in its place with the same ease of movement. She was able to do this because the movable fingers of her hand were brought into play by separate strings.

This particular puppet, seated at the weaving loom, represented the legendary female warrior Hua Mu-lan.

In the second scene, when Mu-lan, in the costume of a warrior, wins a contest with bow and arrow, the tiny hands of the puppet actually tightened the bow string and despatched a real arrow.

The majority of puppeteers in old China were either not very literate or entirely illiterate people, but popular ingenuity and an unbroken centuries-old tradition evolved a puppet 'anatomy' and a technique of construction, which one man alone could never have done no matter how literate or technically skilled he might have been.

In using the term 'centuries-old' I have perhaps made a mistake, since the tradition is really thousands of years old. In a work entitled *The Origins of the Chinese Puppet Theatre*, the author —Sun Kai-ti—when speaking of the first historical documents which contain references to the existence of the puppet theatre in China, begins his enumeration of these with *The Book of Music*. This work was written by Chen Yuan, who lived in the epoch of the Sung Dynasty—eight hundred years ago. But this period evidently has to be increased almost four times over, because when speaking of the puppet theatre Chen Yuan refers to a popular legend concerning a puppet master named Yang Shih who made the first puppets and performed with them at the court of the Chu emperor, Mu-Wang, who reigned in the tenth century B.C., i.e. three thousand years ago.

The legend tells us that on one occasion the Emperor felt that the puppets were winking irreverently at his wives and courtiers. Mu-Wang ordered the puppet master to be put to death, but before the executioner could approach Yang Shih, he quickly slashed his puppets with a knife to prove that they were not really alive. Mu-Wang got over it and allowed Yang Shih to continue performing, but, just to make sure that there would be no further unpleasantness of any kind in future, he forbade his wives to watch any such performances. Sun Kai-ti writes that the custom of not allowing women to witness puppet performances was preserved in feudal China until very recent times.

There is another legend of how the first puppet was invented. This was recorded in the Tang epoch, by Tuan An-chieh, in his book *Notes on Folk Songs*. In this legend we are told how the leader of a nomadic tribe, Khan Modo, laid siege to the city of Pinchen, the residence of the founder of the Han dynasty, Emperor Kao-Tzu. The town was saved by one of the Emperor's courtiers. Knowing that the wife of the Khan was very temperamental, he commanded that a puppet should be made in the form of a beautiful maiden and, with the assistance of some contraption or other, he made it dance on the city wall.

The Khan's wife, noticing the dancer's beauty, and thinking that it was alive, became very perturbed because she thought that, if the town was taken, the Khan would take this beauty as his concubine. In such an event she would lose the Khan's love and good will. The danger seemed to her so great and so real that the terrified wife persuaded her husband to abandon the siege of the town.

Neither of these legends of course reveal the origins of the puppet theatre of China, but their existence is evidence of the fact, that, already in very early times, the puppet theatre was part and parcel of the everyday social life of the people and clearly existed as a popular form of of entertainment. The custom forbidding women to witness puppet performances was in no way connected with the fact that the puppets winked at the Imperial wives, but the mention of this prohibition strengthens the probability of the existence of the puppet theatre in that epoch. The prohibition against women being present at such performances as spectators, arose from the widespread absence of women's rights in the feudal East and was typical not only of old China. In Indonesia for example, until quite recently women were not permitted to watch the shadow theatre from the same side of the screen as men, but only from behind, i.e. from the side where the actual models and the man who operated them were visible.

The difficulty of investigating the origin of the Chinese puppet theatre is increased, because in the Chinese language, performances with masks and puppet performances are both referred to by one and the same name—*Kuei lei hsi*, and it is often impossible to determine whether any old document refers to people in masks or to puppets.

A classification of puppet theatres does however exist in one of these old books and the author enumerates five fundamental forms: the 'portable booth', i.e. glove puppets, 'string puppets', 'powder puppets', 'floating puppets' and 'live puppets'.

I have already described the first two types in sufficient detail. There is not very much more I can say about the other three, and in any case, I know no more than Sun Kai-ti, the author of the book *On the Origins of the Chinese Puppet Theatre*.

'Powder puppets' no longer exist, nor is there any extant description of their construction. These puppets were probably set in motion by some mechanical device, where the dynamic force was provided in the form of a powder explosion, i.e. something like the contemporary combustion engine. We ought therefore to describe these as 'pyrotechnic' puppets.

As for 'floating puppets', the evidence is somewhat greater, but still too meagre for us to imagine what a performance was like. These were constructed in human form, but only from the waist upwards, and rested on cross-shaped or circular wooden bases, which enabled them to float on park lakes.

Sun Kai-ti writes that 'live' puppet performances were characteristic of the Sung epoch only. These were, in fact, children in costume, sitting on the shoulders of grown-ups and imitating the movements of puppets.

He also considers that the shadow theatre is of later origin, and relates it to the Tang epoch, i.e. to the seventh to ninth centuries or slightly later—the period of the Fifth Dynasty, and that it was finally established in the eleventh century.

It would in fact be more correct to refer to the shadow theatre as the 'coloured shadow theatre', since the cut-out figures of asses' skin are semi-transparent and coloured, and moreover, faces, hat ornaments and sometimes costumes are drawn on both sides of the skin. The cut-out is placed close up against the screen and, when immobile, the whole of its surface touches it. The light from a lamp, placed behind the paper or fabric screen, passes through the transparent skin of the cut-out figures on to the screen, on the other side of which the audience watches the performance, where it shows up in remarkable colour and beauty to give the effect of a brilliant, but at the same time slightly subdued, coloured drawing, which is almost animate.

The shadow figure is mobile in the joints of the shoulders, elbows, wrists, thighs and legs and is manipulated by three rods. The main rod, from which the puppet is suspended, is attached to the neck, and the other two are joined to the wrists. The puppeteer brings the puppet out into the illuminated screen area, and holding the main rod in one hand, he manipulates the remaining two with the other, which is of course very difficult, thus causing the puppet to perform certain movements with its arms. If the figure has to stand still, the puppeteer places the main rod so that it leans against the upper part of the screen, which is draped with a coarse material, while the puppet itself rests against the slightly slanting screen. He now has both hands free to manipulate these figures or to introduce others, if need be.

These shadow figures are not very large—generally about twenty, thirty or forty centimetres high. The dimensions of a screen may vary, but as a rule, these too are not very great—about sixty to eighty centimetres high and about a metre or a metre and a half broad. The theatre itself is like a portable booth, inside which is the chief puppeteer himself —the 'upper hand', and his assistants—the 'lower hands'.

The puppet and shadow theatres are very similar to the traditional living theatre in their repertoire, the movements of figures, costumes, facial make-up and musical accompaniment, and there is much which is even identical.

The question arises quite naturally as to which of these came first, which created this repertoire and its form of expression, and who borrowed it all.

There are conflicting points of view on this. Many people consider that the puppet theatre, including the shadow theatre, borrowed the forms of the traditional living theatre in their entirety, while others have arrive at exactly the opposite conclusion and assert that the puppet theatre is the 'ancestor', and the living theatre—the heir and borrower. This is in fact what Sun Kai-ti writes. In support of his hypothesis he draws attention to the fact that the original forms of the classical theatre of the Sung epoch are very similar in their repertoire to those of the puppet theatre, and that many expressive idioms adopted by the living theatre appear to be much more organic and natural in the shadow or puppet theatre. For example, the aside to the audience by a player of the classical theatre on his first appearance on stage, with a clear definitive statement of who he is and what he is about to do, seems to the author to be an atavistic form preserved from the puppet theatre, where it is the puppeteer who gives such information about a character.

Sun Kai-ti also considers that the unchanging design of facial make-up, which at once defines the character of the hero, his social position and his part in the subject matter, is quite natural for puppets, but not necessary for a human actor on the stage.

Finally, he draws attention to the fact that many of the gestures and postures of living actors appear to imitate those of puppets. Particularly characteristic in this connection is the peculiar gait of the Chinese actor, in which the leg, bending at the knee to form a right angle, rises perpendicular to the floor and drops in the same strictly perpendicular way, i.e. there is a resulting movement which is absolutely identical with the movement of a puppet's legs with strings attached to them.

These examples, like the hypothesis itself, are not new. Many theatrical scholars, apart from Chinese, have established the right of the puppet to be regarded as the 'ancestor' of the living actor. The same references to the 'puppet-like' character of the gestures and postures of stage actors can be found in an article by N. Conrad, on the Japanese theatre, which was published in a symposium entitled *The Oriental Theatre*. In this article he asserts that the movements of the Japanese actors of the Kabuki theatre originated in the Dzoruri puppet theatre of Japan.

I am not a theatrical scholar or historian. My more than modest erudition on these questions does not permit me to affirm, nor fundamentally refute these hypotheses; and while it is gratifying to me, as a puppet theatre artist, to think that the puppet is awarded the honour of primogeniture, it does not seem to me to be very probable. The fact that a puppet is a representation of a human being, that is to say derived from a human being, does not permit us to reverse the natural process and push the egg into the chicken. Evidently the matter is much more simple. The history of the theatre, including the puppet theatre, is the history of imitative entertainment. It is as vast as the history of human society. Imitative movements addressed to audiences originally took the form of human dance-pantomimes, in which the performer was always costumed in some way or other, i.e. he endeavoured to define the object he was supposed to represent by his external appearance. I think that the painting of the face preceded the mask, even if only by virtue of the fact that it is easier to smear the face with soot or berry juice and stick a simple feather in the hair, than to carve out a wooden mask with a sharp stone. But this does not mean to say that later on, facial make-up could not have copied the mask, or a masked human—a puppet. The close connection between the puppet theatre and the living theatre, and the influence of one upon the other at a time when they were both becoming established, were natural and organic, since the 'walls', so to speak, dividing the two types of theatre were so thin that a certain amount of mutual influence was unavoidable.

As regards the Chinese theatre in the form in which it now exists, it seems to me it is much easier to postulate the influence of the traditional classical theatre of living actors on the puppet theatre, rather than the other way round. It does not of course follow from this that there are no specific elements of the puppet theatre which indicate an independent development. And indeed when we find a puppet play which is identical with its counterpart on the living stage, we cannot be absolutely certain that it has jumped as it were from the footlights of the living theatre on to the puppet stage. We cannot be certain because its subject matter did not originate in the theatre but had its roots in the literary and folk epics. The majority of the plays of both theatres originate in the very same folk legends and novels, e.g., *The Three Kingdoms*, *Journeys to the West* and *The River Creeks*.

In April 1955, more than two hundred people from all over China came to Peking for the All Chinese Festival of Puppet and Shadow Theatres. For the first time in the whole history of Chinese puppetry, specialists in this art from the various provinces of China were able to meet; they saw each other's performances and methods of work and judged each other's standard of craftsmanship, all of which was regarded as important and necessary. The Ministry of Culture of the Chinese People's Republic published information on the festival, in which brief details were given of each theatre, biographies of the actors and their repertoires and the subject matter of individual plays. An analysis of this published material could in itself form the subject of major research. This is not within my power, but certain general, and, as it seems to me, very fundamental conclusions can be drawn without any danger of falling into error.

First of all it is clear that the puppet and shadow theatres have a greater variety of forms than the traditional living theatre. And this is quite natural. After all, although the local forms of the traditional theatre may differ from one another from the point of view of dialect, melodies used, orchestration and dramatic presentation of the subject, they in no way differ in fundamental method, i.e. in their medium of theatrical expression. But the puppet and shadow theatres which are distinguished in exactly the same way by local forms of dialect, music, orchestration and subject presentation, are further sub-divided inside each local form by characteristics based on the medium of expression. Some theatres use string puppets, others glove puppets, a third group uses rod puppets and finally there are theatres which use wire puppets. I unexpectedly came across this last method of puppet manipulation, which was hitherto unknown to me, in the printed matter of the Festival and in photographs. Wire puppets are operated not from above or below, but from behind, through a wide gap in the back cloth, covered by a loosely hanging material. This is, so to speak, a variant of rod manipulation, but the rods—or more correctly the wires—are not attached to the waist, legs and arms of the puppet vertically, but horizontally. Unfortunately I did not see any performances where this method was used and I only grasped the details of their construction by a close examination of photographs.

Thus the Chinese puppet theatre employs almost all forms of puppetry which exist in other countries.

The traditional puppet theatres of China, divided as they are by visual characteristics into theatres using different methods of presentation and puppet construction, and by generic characteristics into different local forms, represent a kind of family which is even more variegated than that of the living theatres. And if the Chinese reckon to have more than two hundred different theatrical forms of the latter, then this figure should be at least doubled for the puppet theatre.

For example, the Chekian string puppet theatre differs from the same kind of puppet theatre in the province of Shensi, and both of these differ from theatres using the same kind of puppets in the provinces of Kuantung or Western Fukien; likewise the shadow theatres in the province of Chekiang differ from the Kuangtung shadow theatres, while they in turn differ from the theatres in Hunan, Hopei, Shantung, Shensi and Heilungkiang.

But in each of the provinces mentioned there are several theatres of each type. For example, in 1954, in one district alone—Shanhan in Western Fukien—there were fifty troupes of actors using string puppets. At the same time, in the southern part alone of the same province of Fukien, there were eleven collectives performing with glove puppets. In the whole of China there are more than one thousand puppet and shadow theatres.

Among the two hundred people who arrived in Peking for

the Festival, there were of course people of varied ability and differing degrees of talent; but professional skill, genuine professional skill, was displayed by practically all of them. They had all been practising not just for a few years, but for decades, and had performed in the streets and squares of towns and villages not just hundreds of times but thousands of times.

This is obvious from the report on the Festival which gives information about some of the chief performers who received prizes and awards.

Here is some information about a few of them in very abbreviated form:

CHIU PI-SHU. An actor of one of the collectives of the Western Fukien string puppet theatre and a native of the district of Shanhan—the cradle of the Western Fukien form of puppet theatres. Age 62. Has been performing with puppets for 52 years.

WEN PO-YÜN. An actor of the Haining shadow theatre. Age 51. Has been performing since he was 15 and learned his art from his father and grandfather.

YANG SHENG. An actor of the Southern Fukien glove puppet theatre. Four generations of his family have been engaged in this profession and he himself began performing at the age of 10.

WANG HSIAO-CHIANG. An actor of the Keyang string puppet theatre. Age 63. Has been performing since he was 9. Illiterate. But knows more than 100 roles.

WEN CHUNG-HSIE. An actor-musician of the same theatre. Also illiterate. Since he was 12 has been playing the 'huchin'. Now first 'huchin' in the theatre orchestra. [A Chinese two-string fiddle. *Trans.*] He knows the texts of 50 plays and the same number of folk melodies by heart. When a group of Shensi musicians who were collecting folk songs decided to write these melodies down, Wen Chung-hsie had to play for 70 days running.

What kind of plays were brought to Peking by the puppet and shadow theatres of China?

The answer to this question is provided by the printed material of the Festival, which gives not only the names of all the fifty-five plays performed in Peking, but also a description of their contents.

Much of the repertoire of these theatres is devoted to heroism, the theme of the struggle for independence of the people, its unity and prosperity, i.e. the struggle with foreign invaders, traitors, depraved and unjust emperors, evil and greedy land-owners, stupid and conceited Ministers, puffed-up officials and generals—in short, with all the enemies of the Chinese people, internal and external.

Among the heroic plays there are a great many dramatizations of separate chapters or complete episodes from *The Three Kingdoms* and *The River Creeks.*

The Southern Fukien puppet theatre performed a play entitled *Tsien Han steals a letter.* All the characters in this play—Chu-yui a general of the kingdom of Wu, and his opponent Tsien Gan, one of the counsellors of General Tsao-Tsao, and finally Tsao-tsao himself—are heroes of *The Three Kingdoms.*

The Northern Szechuan puppet theatre using rod puppets, performed two plays from *The Three Kingdoms,—Burning Puyang* and *The Capture of Pan-de.*

Whereas in the play *Burning Puyang* the outcome of the struggle is decided by the element of fire, in *The Capture of Pan-de* it is the element of water which is decisive. It is worth while relating the subject of this play.

General Huan-yü has laid siege to the town of Fangchen. In order to relieve the garrison, Tsao-tsao sends troops under the command of Yü-chin, and among them is the brave and strong warrior Pan-de, who fights boldly in the vanguard.

At first Huan-yü's campaign goes badly and he himself is even wounded in the shoulder by a well-aimed arrow from Pan-de. Autumn comes and when the rains have swollen the river into a torrent, Huan-yü dams up the stream with a vast number of sandbags. There has been no actual fighting for a considerable time. The enemy's vigilance has slackened and his advanced posts are taken. On a dark night when the wind is blowing particularly strongly towards the enemy, Huan-yü gives the order to destroy the dam, whereupon the pent-up waters surge into the sleeping camp. Yü-chin and Pan-de take refuge on a hillock which soon becomes an island, but even here they are not safe, and detachments of Huan-yü's troops land on the hillock from all sides in four large boats. Yü-chin is taken prisoner, but Pan-de still tries to escape from the enemy in a small boat. The soldiers of one of Huan-yü's commanders, Chu-tsien, manage to overtake him and sink his boat. Undaunted, Pan-de tries to swim ashore, but Chu-tsien plunges into the water after him and it is here that the finale of the struggle between the two enemies takes place.

Pan-de is taken prisoner and thus the victory over Tsao-tsao is complete, but, as you see, the enemy in this play, as in many other heroic Chinese plays, is depicted as strong, bold and dangerous, i.e. the kind of person in the struggle against whom the strength and boldness of a positive hero can be displayed and proved. The puppet figure of Pan-de has red moustaches because in the traditional Chinese theatre, red make-up signifies boldness, while Chu-tsien's are black—the colour of honesty.

The Szechuan theatre also took part in the Festival using 'large' puppets—which according to the Festival programme are very rarely met with. They are approximately the size of a human being, and those representing soldiers are particularly large. This theatre performed a play entitled *On the Fen min shan mountain.* Its subject matter, taken from the 92nd chapter of *The Three Kingdoms*, tells how Chao yün defeated an army of 8,000 led by five very experienced and bold generals.

But whereas all the plays taken from *The Three Kingdoms* are concerned with military heroism, the majority of those taken from *The River Creeks* depict social heroism, and their fundamental theme is the struggle against social injustice. I should no doubt weary the reader if I were to relate the subject matter of all these plays from *The River Creeks* in detail, but so as to give some idea of them, it will suffice to describe the finale of the play *Tamingfu*, which was performed by the West Fukien puppet theatre.

In order to free a man who has been unjustly imprisoned, one of the '108 heroes' living in the legendary mountains orders the rebels to infiltrate into the town of Tamingfu during the Lantern Festival. Once inside, they set fire to the *Palace of the Birch Clouds*, where all the eminent people of the town have gathered; they destroy the garrison prison, free the arrested man and his wife and distribute the property of the prison governor among the poor.

No less a degree of social indignation is evident in the play *The Mountain with Forty Legs* performed by the Haiping shadow theatre from the province of Cheking. In this play the rebels make very short work of a depraved monk who was intent on his forcing his attentions on a poor peasant girl.

The puppet theatre of Shensi province performed a play entitled *K'uai ho lin*. The hero, Wu sung, despite the fact that he has endured forty strokes of the birch, branding and banishment, nevertheless carries on the struggle against injustice and stands up for everyone who falls victim to it.

Many puppet and shadow theatres performed plays based on subjects taken from *Journeys to the West*. In genre these plays can be grouped together with the heroic and the satirical. Mayakovsky would probably have used the term 'heroic-comedy' to describe them. This humorous satire arises from the fact that the central figure in every play is the Monkey King, Sung Wu-k'un.

For example, the Haiping shadow theatre performed *Uproar*

in the Sea Kingdom, one of the initial episodes of the novel, in which Sung Wu-k'un wins a magic needle from the Tsar of the Ocean, after fighting with three dragons—white, black and red.

The shadow theatre of the province of Heilungkiang showed *Uproar in the Palace of Heaven*, in which Sung Wu-k'un first of all eats up all the 'peaches of immortality' in the palace garden, then drinks all the 'wine of immortality' which had been prepared for a feast of the Gods, and swallows pills prepared by the God 'Daos' for protection against fire.

I have already mentioned the satirical play *Chu Pa-chieh and the Maiden*, in which Sung Wu-k'un turns into a beautiful maiden and tricks a monk, but I would like to tell you about a play taken from *Journeys to the West*, entitled *The mountain of fiery tongues*, in which romantic heroism and buffoonery are introduced in, as it seems to me, a very marked way. This play was performed at the Festival by both the Szechuan puppet theatre and the Hunan shadow theatre. Here, in brief, is how the play develops in the shadow theatre.

While on a journey, a monk and his companions find their path blocked by a mountain. It is impossible to go round it and to cross it is even more difficult, since flames are belching forth from its summit. Sung Wu-k'un therefore sets out to pay a visit to the evil spirit, Niu-mo, to get a 'wind fan' from him. Niu-mo deceives Sung Wu-k'un and instead of a 'wind fan' for blowing out the flames, he gives him a 'fire fan'. Having discovered the trick, Sung Wu-k'un, who was able as you may remember, to turn himself into anything he pleased, assumes the form of Niu-mo so that he can gain access to the latter's wife—the Princess of the Iron Fan. But apparently Niu-mo too is capable of turning himself into anything at will. He becomes a bull and attacks his double. Sung Wu-k'un then turns himself into a reed and allows the bull to eat him. Once inside the bull's stomach Sung Wu-k'un begins to make a frightful disturbance which gives the bull a terrible stomach-ache. So as finally to defeat Niu-mo, Sung Wu-k'un tiess a string round his heart, whereupon it stops beating. Niu-mo surrenders and makes a passage for the travellers over 'The Mountain of Fiery Tongues'.

The majority of plays performed at the Festival were devoted to the lot of women. Very often in these plays it is the woman herself who fights for her own rights, while in other cases it is her husband, father, brother or fiancé who fights for her honour and happiness.

This might appear at first to be unusual, but because women in feudal China had no rights and were almost slaves, they became the heroines of many popular plays. In fact, the material for these tragic and heroic themes was taken straight from life—life as it was in every village and home, in a young woman's own home and in that of her fiancé's family to whom she was sold. Love and the feelings of the heart had no place whatsoever within the legal framework of a forced marriage, and popular art naturally reflected this.

Two plays were performed at the Festival depicting the legendary prisoner in the pagoda of Lei Feng ta—the heroic White Serpent, as a young girl in love, a faithful wife and tender mother. The puppet theatre from the province of Kiangsu played *The theft of the miraculous grass*, which White Serpent acquires in order to cure her lover; and the Heilungkiang shadow theatre showed *The Flooding of the Monastery of the Golden Mountain*—an episode in which, White Serpent already pregnant, goes to battle against the 'Powers of Heaven' who have taken her husband away from her.

But White Serpent is not the only clever, bold warrior depicted on the stage of the Chinese puppet theatre. Mu-lan, about whom I saw a play in Shanghai, is just as brave and skilful in battle; and Shao-yü-lan, who at the head of an army of many thousands which she has mustered, goes forth to the defence of her husband who has been taken prisoner. This play was performed at the Festival by the shadow theatre from Hopei province.

But it is not only in war that a woman has to resort to arms. Sometimes she is obliged to do so on her wedding night in order to defend her honour. In the play *Han Miao Chien*, performed at the Festival by the wire puppet theatre from the province of Fukien, the heroine, who had been forcibly married off to a man she hated, kills him as soon as they are alone together after the wedding feast.

Occasionally some stranger may come to the defence of a weak woman. The same theatre performed a play about Sun Tsui-e, who twice saves a girl named Pai Yü-shuang. On the first occasion she drags her out of a river which she has thrown herself into, so that she would not have to marry a man she did not love, and on the second occasion when she realizes that she cannot save the girl's life unless she saves her from a forced marriage, she herself dons the wedding garments, goes in to the husband and kills him.

Many of the plays devoted to the fate of women end sadly. For example, the play *Meeting in a hotel*, performed by the puppet theatre from Shensi province, ends with a sad parting of lovers who are not destined to be happy because they are separated for ever by the caprice of others. The play *A legal scandal*, presented by the Shensi puppet theatre ends with the suicide of the heroine, as is also the case in *The return of Chu Shen*, presented by the Heiyang theatre.

There are of course numerous endings which are not only 'heroically victorious', but simply jolly and humorous. Social criticism and seriousness, however, are never absent from these plays.

In this connection, *The Flour Jar* performed by the shadow and rod puppet theatres of Hunan province, is very typical.

In the first place this play is interesting because the heroine is a prostitute, but nevertheless she has the complete sympathy of the audience. This is quite natural since she is a person who is not only oppressed but also fighting for her freedom. She goes to the office of the Chief Area Administrator and asks his permission to leave the brothel and marry the man she loves. The official gives his permission, but on the day of the wedding he comes to the house of the newly-weds to amuse himself with the bride. He regards her, as before, as a prostitute and does not expect a refusal. Pretending that she wishes to conceal him from her husband, the wife suggests that her guest should hide in a large earthenware flour jar; when her husband comes in she tells him who is hidden in the house and where. To the great joy of the faithful wife, the husband beats the official, now covered in flour, with a thick stick and throws him ignominiously out of the house.

The majority of the plays of the puppet and shadow theatre which I have described are, as I have already said, also performed in the living theatre and correspond, if not in text, in theme and subject matter.

Does this mean that the shadow and puppet theatres simply copy the productions of the living theatre? No, it does not. If this was the case, then neither the puppet nor the shadow theatre could have become so widely diffused throughout the country or have existed for so many years.

For audiences, both the shadow and puppet theatres have their own intrinsic artistic value, providing a particular aesthetic pleasure. This is not just because of the subject matter of the plays or the virtuosity of the puppeteers, but because of the additional elements of theatrical expression which are organically peculiar to these theatres, i.e. because of the different expressive media and possibilities in the puppet theatre, the shadow theatre and the living theatre.

I have just mentioned the performance by the Heilungkiang shadow theatre of *The Flooding of the Monastery of the Golden Mountain*. I was not present on this occasion and have not seen this production, but I have seen the play—more correctly, its subject matter—performed by living actors—students of the School of Classical Drama in Peking, and also by one of the string puppet theatres of Eastern China.

These two performances were quite different, that is in their method of expression and treatment.

Against the 'Powers of Heaven' who are on the side of the monks, White Serpent summons the 'Powers of Water'—the soldiers of the underwater kingdom, among whom are fish, crabs and tortoises. In the performance by the living theatre these semi-fantastic creatures were defined outwardly by simple costume effects. The actors, dressed in blue costumes, wore hats shaped like crabs, fish and tortoises, while the water was represented by lengths of blue silk with waves drawn on them.

But how was all this depicted in the puppet theatre?

We were in Shanghai one evening in the middle of December. It was very dark, the weather was damp and the rain was beginning to turn to snow. A small theatre, or to be more correct—a stage, flood-lit in front, stood under the open sky on a raised platform. We were given umbrellas and we sat down on a wooden bench right in front of the stage. It was like a small palace of carved wood, studded here and there with precious stones and decorated with cobalt, cinebar, gold and silver, and the whole was sprinkled with pearls of fine rain. This glittering rain imparted a fairy-tale appearance to the stage. I felt it would be a great pity if the rain were to spoil this wonderful 'large toy'.

To the sound of gongs, two beautiful ladies appeared, one in white and the other in blue—the two sisters, White Serpent and Blue Serpent. A monk then made his appearance on the stage. White Serpent coaxed, persuaded and demanded that the monastery should give her back her husband, but entreaties, persuasion and even threats are of no avail. Therefore she would have to fight—there was no other way out. She then summons the 'Powers of Water' to aid her.

Up to this point the internal development of the action had differed from what we had seen in the living theatre only in so far as these were puppets and not real people. Their movements were determined by their particular construction, but the moment the battle began, the special peculiarities and possibilities of the puppet theatre came into play. The stage was filled with crabs, tortoises and fish, i.e. with characters which cannot be shown on the living stage, no matter how they may be costumed or their faces painted. And at the end when, according to the story, the water was supposed to flood the 'Monastery of the Golden Mountain', fifteen fountains began to play. My anxiety lest the rain should spoil the precious stage frontage was clearly unfounded. I had forgotten about the qualities of Chinese lacquer which preserves its colour and the faultless smoothness of its surface for hundreds of years despite rain, snow, frost and scorching winds.

But the most important thing was not, of course, the quality of the lacquer, but the fact that the characters and the treatment of the finale were not the same as in the living theatre, and belonged intrinsically to the puppet theatre. This was also the case in the play *Mu lan* which was being shown by another puppet theatre that same evening. In this play there is an episode when Mu lan jumps on a horse. In the traditional human theatre, the horse in this case would have been suggested only by a riding whip in the actor's hands. Here in the puppet theatre there was no mere whip, but a horse on which the heroine could sit and gallop wherever she pleased. So here too, although the play corresponded with the same play as produced in the ordinary theatre, the media of expression were in many cases considerably different. By being able to depict a horse or a boat by means of a puppet or a shadow, there was no need to use a mere whip or a paddle.

As for stage scenery—in the traditional puppet theatres of China as in the living theatre, it is as a rule non-existent. In the shadow theatre, where a definition of the place of action can perhaps be created more easily, there are not only cut-out patterns of tables and chairs, but vases of flowers, trees and clouds. During changes of scenery, more often than not the lighted screen is not extinguished or closed over. The shadows of the wires by which the puppets are operated are, although dimly seen, nevertheless visible; but this does not worry anyone, as the spectators are used to it. Nor are people in any way perturbed or surprised when the large shadows of human hands appear during changes of scenery, i.e. when a table is being replaced by a chair or a cloud by a tree. Audience reaction to the change of scenery in the shadow theatre is the same as that during a performance in the theatre of musical drama when furniture is being moved.

Thus, although the traditional shadow and puppet theatres of China are often very similar to the traditional Chinese living theatre from the point of view of the names and subject matter of plays, in costume effects and facial make-up, they are distinguished from it by those additional means of expression peculiar to puppets and shadow puppets.

This fact seems to me very significant, since it suggests a single origin for the different forms of the popular Chinese theatre, while at the same time indicating that puppets and shadows developed independently, and even though they are similar in many ways to the living theatre, they at any rate do not imitate it.

This explains why plays are performed in the puppet theatre and shadow theatre which cannot be found in the repertoire of other theatres. For example, the description I gave of the short play *Chu Pa-chieh and the Maiden*, in which the 'monk-pig' carried on his back Sung Wü k'un, who turns into a young woman, is evidently only performed in the puppet theatre, since it would not only be difficult for a living actor to carry another person on his back for a long time, but it would be rather pointless. In such a case not only would Chu Pa-chieh get rather tired, but the actor playing the part too, and the audience would not so much laugh at the faltering steps of the stupid monk, as they would pity the poor tired actor or else be astonished at his endurance.

It is only in the puppet theatre that the play about the stupid peasant who is swallowed by a tiger is performed. Such a subject could never arise in an author's mind if he was presenting living people as the characters, and evidently it is easier for people who deal with puppets to think up such things.

In my own personal repertoire there is a number in which a tiger eats up a boasting lion tamer. To tell the truth, I thought it was only in my act that a tiger performs this trick, which is not really very difficult, but is very funny, and I was flabbergasted when I saw exactly the same thing being done by the Chinese puppeteer Yuan Fen-ku in Peking. And, indeed, Yuan Fen-ku was evidently no less surprised when I showed him my puppets after his performance and demonstrated my number with the tiger. We introduced the two tigers to each other, one, hundreds of years old, and the other—only ten.

Another typical play is *The Crane and the Tortoise*, performed at the Festival by the Hunan shadow theatre. This is, in fact, a 'fable-play'. A boastful white crane who is confident that he can fly up into the air whenever he pleases, begins to mock a tortoise, jumps on to its back and pecks it with his large beak. But he is punished for his bad behaviour. The tortoise gnaws through the crane's throat. One has only to imagine the behaviour of the crane and the tortoise and it immediately becomes clear that it is in the shadow theatre that the physical actions of such characters and the characters themselves can best be expressed, and certainly not in the living theatre.

This same theatre presented two other fable-plays—*The Greedy Monkey* and *The Two Friends*. In the first play, a young monkey which comes across a water melon, throws away some peaches it has gathered, but when it sees a large pumpkin, it discards the melon, only to find that it cannot carry the huge pumpkin, which falls into a river. In *The Two Friends*, a clever bear rescues his rather stupid friend—a monkey—by turning over a huge village bell under which the monkey is imprisoned; delighted with the beauty and strength of its sound, the monkey had clung to the clanger and begun swinging back and forth on it until finally the bell fell down.

As you see, these two productions are also quite natural for the shadow theatre, and the idea of presenting such subjects in a theatre arose from the specific character and possibilities of the puppet theatre.

The contemporary fable-play *The Builder Fox* was played by the Southern Fukien puppet theatre. The chief of the poultry yard, an old lion, appoints a donkey as book-keeper, and the donkey in turn charges the fox with the erection of the chicken houses, whereupon the fox devours the chickens and runs away.

This was not the only contemporary play shown at the Festival, and in any case the word 'contemporary', particularly as applied to a play in the Chinese theatre, is not necessarily restricted to the formal subject matter alone, but can be applied to a play which conjures up actual contemporary associations for the audience.

These echoes from the past are just as much in evidence in the puppet and shadow theatre as they are in the theatre of musical drama.

At the same time there are also puppet plays written by contemporary authors on present-day themes. Such for example is the play *New Yangko*, depicting the Festival of the New Year, or *The Marriage of Hsiao-erh-hei*—a comedy in which the old and new forms of marriage are contrasted. Both of these plays were presented by the Peking puppet theatre, while the Kwantung string puppet theatre presented *Fan shu shan*, a play dealing with land reforms.

My meeting with the puppeteers from Eastern China, at which I saw both *The Flooding of the Monastery of the Golden Mountain* and *Mu lan*, went on for two days running, for many hours each day, as the Chinese comrades wanted not only to see my puppets but to find out as much as possible about Soviet puppet theatres. I, in turn, questioned them as much as I could about the puppet theatres of China, but I was mainly interested in seeing their performances, particularly as they were being shown by different theatre groups.

Apart from the two theatres playing with string puppets there were others using rod and glove puppets. Moreover, the performances of these theatres were given not by one man only, as is the case with the 'portable booth', but by several actors. Unfortunately I did not write down the names of the two plays they performed and I cannot now remember them. In the first, which was performed with rod puppets, a rich villain deceives a young girl and she dies; and, in the comedy played by small glove puppets, a wicked and very stupid landowner persecutes a young peasant girl. Even now I cannot forget the consummate artistry displayed by this actor who played the role of the licentious fool. Without any forcing whatsoever, he was completely faithful to the context of the action, and imbued the play with a mass of subtly observed everyday truths, which indicated real acting talent and enabled him to make the conventional appear unconventional.

But I was absolutely astonished when I witnessed a performance given by school-children. On the playboard I saw a hare, then a hunter, then a cat and after a few minutes had elapsed I realized that they were performing George Landau's play *The Hare and the Cat*, which had been first produced in our own theatre. The whole play, from start to finish, was performed exactly as we do it ourselves. How surprising and pleasant it was to see the heroes of our Soviet fable-fairy tale in Shanghai.

This was not an isolated case. In Peking the Chinese Puppet Art Theatre performs the play *Dear Little Duckling*. This, too, came from our theatre, but by a somewhat devious route. Some years ago we produced a play by Nina Gernet and Tatyana Gurevich entitled *The Gosling*. This is a short, funny but very touching play. There are only four characters in it: the girl Alenka—played by a living actress, a gosling, a hedgehog and a fox. This play was taken from us and performed by one of the Czech puppet theatres, who slightly altered it, and the 'gosling' for some reason or other became a 'duckling'. The Chinese then borrowed it from the Czechs and called it *Dear Little Duckling*.

This same theatre also performs the Russian folk tale 'The Turnip', and on Chekhov's jubilee they produced a dramatization of the tale 'The Chameleon'.

The Chinese Puppet Art Theatre grew from a small children's group of puppeteers attached to the Peking Juvenile Arts Theatre. The director of this theatre, Wu Hsueh, introduced me to my young colleagues and I showed them my puppets and told them about the Soviet theatre. All these 12–15-year-old black-eyed lads and lasses have grown up and are now young actors and actresses of one of the first State Puppet Theatres in China which has grown up along with them.

What other plays does this theatre produce apart from those I have already mentioned? How was its repertoire established? This is not only interesting but typical of the great process of the development and growth of theatrical culture in modern China.

A troupe of popular puppeteers from the province of Hunan were invited to Peking to teach their art to the young actors and pass on to them a part of their own repertoire. As a result of this, the classical play *Luhuatan* was included in the repertoire of the Chinese Puppet Art Theatre. This is an episode from *The Three Kingdoms.*

The Peking theatre also produced another classical puppet play, which I have already described. In this theatre it is called *Chu Pa-chieh carries a lady on his back.*

In establishing its repertoire, therefore, the Chinese Puppet Theatre makes use of three sources: plays or dramatized versions of works by dramatists on contemporary themes and subjects, classical plays—the subjects of which are of interest to contemporary audiences, and finally, plays from foreign puppet theatres, including plays performed in the puppet theatres of the Soviet Union.

The puppet theatre in Peking is not the only State Puppet Theatre in China.

State aid is also made available to a puppet theatre group attached to the Shanghai Committee for the Defence of Children, and to the puppet theatre of the Central Academy of Fine Arts and many others.

The renaissance of the art of the puppet theatre of China has only just begun and it is difficult to see how it will develop. But one thing at any rate is important. In very early times the puppet theatre in China was developed to a greater extent than it was in any other country; nowhere were its forms and methods so varied. But towards the end of the nineteenth century and the beginning of the twentieth century, the great art of the puppet theatre began to fall into degeneracy and decay. It might well have disappeared entirely if the revolution had not revealed and unleashed the whole creative power of this great nation. Questions of culture became fundamental questions of the day. The theatre, including the puppet theatre, became part of a singular and powerful development of art serving the people, and actors, including puppeteers, became respected members of society.

To a certain extent this process was analogous to that which took place in our country.

The traditional Petrushka of old Russia also died out as a basic form of the puppet theatre at the beginning of the twentieth century. The October Revolution opened up new possibilities for the theatres of our country, and puppet theatres immediately sprang up in Moscow, Leningrad, Kiev and Kharkov.

When the State Central Puppet Theatre was organized in Moscow in 1931, we invited our oldest folk-puppeteer, Ivan Finogenevich Zaitsev, to come and work with us. At that time he was already more than seventy. He had been performing for many decades, showing his Petrushka and string puppets in towns and villages, in covered fair booths and even in squares, streets and courtyards in the open air. In the course of his long life, this illiterate folk artist of remarkable talent had heard the happy laughter of hundreds of thousands of spectators and experienced that pleasure which springs from artistic success; but before the Revolution he had never had the full respect which his great labours deserved. Even the money he received for his efforts was more often than not dropped into his hat or simply thrown from a window on to a cobbled street.

It was only after the Revolution that he was given a job with a regular income, and for the first time in his life he was conscious not only of the recognition and respect of all the people around him but also of the great value which was attached to the work which the government had provided for him, as being useful and necessary.

Ivan F. Zaitsev, who passed on to us a great heritage of folk art, was the first actor of the puppet theatres of the Soviet Union to receive the title of Honoured Artist of the Republic.

Whenever I look through the printed material of the Peking Puppet Festival and read the biographies of the puppeteers who demonstrated the magnificent art of their people there, I invariably think of Ivan F. Zaitsev. How many old puppeteers there are in this list, just like him, who have lived on into these happier times, so that their labour and their profession, which were previously looked down upon, are now honoured and respected! How many puppeteers there are who have received awards, diplomas, honoured titles and become teachers and directors of theatres!

In December 1956, when the Russian edition of this book was already set up in type and the printing house began sending me the first galley proofs, a group of Chinese puppet actors came to Moscow. They were on their way home to China after a tour of Czechoslovakia and Poland, and therefore they only presented a few performances in the Central House of Art Workers and in the House of the All Russian Actors' Society in Moscow. Unfortunately I am no longer able to expand this account sufficiently to describe in detail all that the Chinese puppeteers showed us, but I shall nevertheless try to describe briefly what seems to me to be particularly important.

First of all, it is characteristic that there were representatives of three theatres in this group of puppeteers, and it reflects very exactly the evolutionary process which is now taking place in the Chinese puppet theatre. This is the process of passing on to young actors the experience of professional folk puppeteers who have devoted decades of their lives to the art of the puppet or shadow theatre.

In this group, the younger actors were from the Peking theatre and either played secondary roles or assisted their older comrades, i.e. by handing them glove puppets or clearing them away after use, or preparing string puppets for their appearance on stage. The experienced, highly qualified folk puppeteers, Yang Shen and Chen nan tien, completely astonished the audience with their artistry. They performed the play *Lei wan chung kills a tiger*. The tiny glove puppets looked just like living creatures; their movements were so strikingly real and rhythmical and they fought so wonderfully. The whole play was pervaded with remarkable humour. The play is a heroic one and the actual killing of the tiger is shown as a great exploit, but this does not prevent the tiger from scratching itself, catching a flea on its back paw or sighing humorously from weariness.

It lasted for half an hour, but the attention of the audience did not falter for a single second. Yang Shen and Chen nan tien have been performing for more than thirty years now and first took puppets in their hands when they were children. In the play they showed us, every movement was perfect and there was true-to-life behaviour in every second of the action, because the operative skill of the actors was enlivened by great acting talent and genuine emotion, without which their skill could not have been demonstrated to the best advantage.

A play by Hsueh Chuang Hua, director of the string puppet theatre from the province of Fukien, was also remarkable for its artistry and skill, but perhaps I was most highly impressed by two short pantomime-plays performed by the shadow theatre. In one of these, the heroes were a crane and a tortoise, and in the other a monkey and a bear. These are the two fable-plays which I have already mentioned, but I have previously only described them on the basis of what I had gathered from the Festival programme. In Moscow I actually saw them and they turned out to be quite remarkable.

Our most outstanding directors and actors—Kedrov, Zavadskii, Torporkov, Livanov, Bryantsev and Yutkevich—were sitting in the auditorium—all grown-up people, greatly experienced in their art and who are not easily surprised or amazed. But nevertheless they were simply captivated by what they saw.

It is very difficult, literally impossible, to explain to readers in words what exactly it was in these fables which so impressed the audience. After all, their content, as you remember, is very simple. A crane proceeds to bully a tortoise, regarding it as an absolutely insignificant and helpless creature. But levity and bragging are punished. The tortoise seizes its opportunity and gnaws through the crane's throat. This was one of the short plays.

The second is even simpler. A monkey makes friends with a bear. While playing about, it hangs on to the clanger of a bell and begins to swing to and fro. The bell falls, covering the monkey, and the bear, with some difficulty, pushes the bell over and frees his friend.

There is not a single spoken word in either of these plays. How long can a scene possibly last, which consists only of a crane trying to peck a tortoise on the head or tail? Apparently it can be made to last for the whole of seven minutes! And for seven whole minutes the audience is in fits of laughter.

Every actor and director knows that a seven-minute scene is fairly long. What happened during these seven minutes? Clever tricks? Eccentric movements? No—there was no eccentricity here at all. Not a single trick! One would have thought that in such a scene there would be nothing to laugh at really, but nevertheless the laughter did not die down and the audience even burst into applause. It was simply because of the striking life-like reality and correctness of every movement made by the crane and the tortoise.

How often we have seen a monkey scratching itself, in the theatre or in cartoon films! We have become used to it and it would seem that such an action could no longer surprise or delight anyone.

In the pantomime *The Two Friends* the monkey scratches itself, then it scratches the bear's chest, stomach and back and teaches the bear how to scratch her neck and chest. And in the movements of the monkey's dark silhouette there was such absolute truth, such unity of action with her partner, that here too the whole auditorium smiled, laughed and applauded almost every five or ten seconds. This play was performed by the actors, Wu chiu shen, Tang te kuei and Wang Fu-shen, and the figures were cut out and constructed by one of the most famous makers of shadow figures of the province of Hunan—Ho tai Sheng.

At the end of the performances there was a meeting between the Soviet puppeteers and their professional colleagues—the Chinese puppeteers. Our guests were bombarded with questions. How many rehearsals had been necessary to work out each movement of the monkey and the bear in such detail? Apparently these few minutes of action had been rehearsed for a month, during which time all the movements were perfected, and a further twenty-four rehearsals were carried out to co-ordinate these physical movements with the musical accompaniment. All performances in the Chinese puppet and shadow theatre have constant musical accompaniment.

The Soviet puppeteers also asked how long it takes to make string and glove puppets and how much such puppets would cost if they have movable eyes, lips and fingers and if the detailed embroidery of the costumes is specially done with precious stones, etc.

The Director of the troupe, a dramatist and teacher of acting and directing, of the Institute of Theatrical Art in Peking, comrade Chu Hsin nan, replied: 'These puppets are very expensive. While in use, they are puppet-actors, and when not in use, we have to regard them as valuable museum pieces. Many of the puppets you have seen are a hundred or more years old. Even some of the recently made puppets can be regarded as works of art in themselves, because of the detailed costume decorations, the art of the sculptor or carver, and even the material they are made of. They are in fact carved from special, very expensive, literally precious wood.'

On hearing this reply, I was once more convinced that there are no 'ordinary props' and no 'simple window-dressing' in the Chinese theatre since every object is primarily a work of art in itself.

We saw our guests off from the Yaroslavl station; we laughed, sang songs, shook each other by the hand, waved our handkerchiefs and hats and parted fully confident that we must surely meet again.

Good-bye for now, dear colleagues! To all of you—my comrades in the profession I love so much, and all who are carefully passing on the heritage of our art to the younger generation, and to you, the younger actors who carry it forward—my best wishes for your success in developing all that is best in and has preserved the living tradition of popular art, and in building in these auspicious times the new China of to-day!

1. Behind the scenes in the Tsuan-chu theatre (Fukien province).

2. *New Yangko*. Chinese Art Puppet Theatre.

3. A 'portable booth'.

4. The stage of a 'portable booth'.

5. Chen nan tien, a puppeteer from the province of Fukien.

6. Puppeteer Shen from the town of Chendu.

7. Puppet Master Syui Lien-sui.

8. Sui Sien and White Serpent. Glove puppets made by People's Master Tsien Tsia-chu.

9. A string puppet writing.

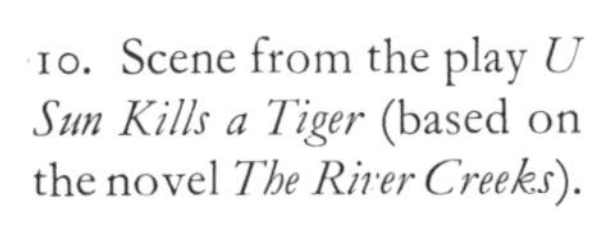

10. Scene from the play *U Sun Kills a Tiger* (based on the novel *The River Creeks*).

11. Sung Wu-k'un and Chu Pa-chieh. Small rod puppets.

12. Rod puppets.

13. String puppet—a 'military commander'.

14. An eighteenth-century rod puppet.

15. Glove puppets.

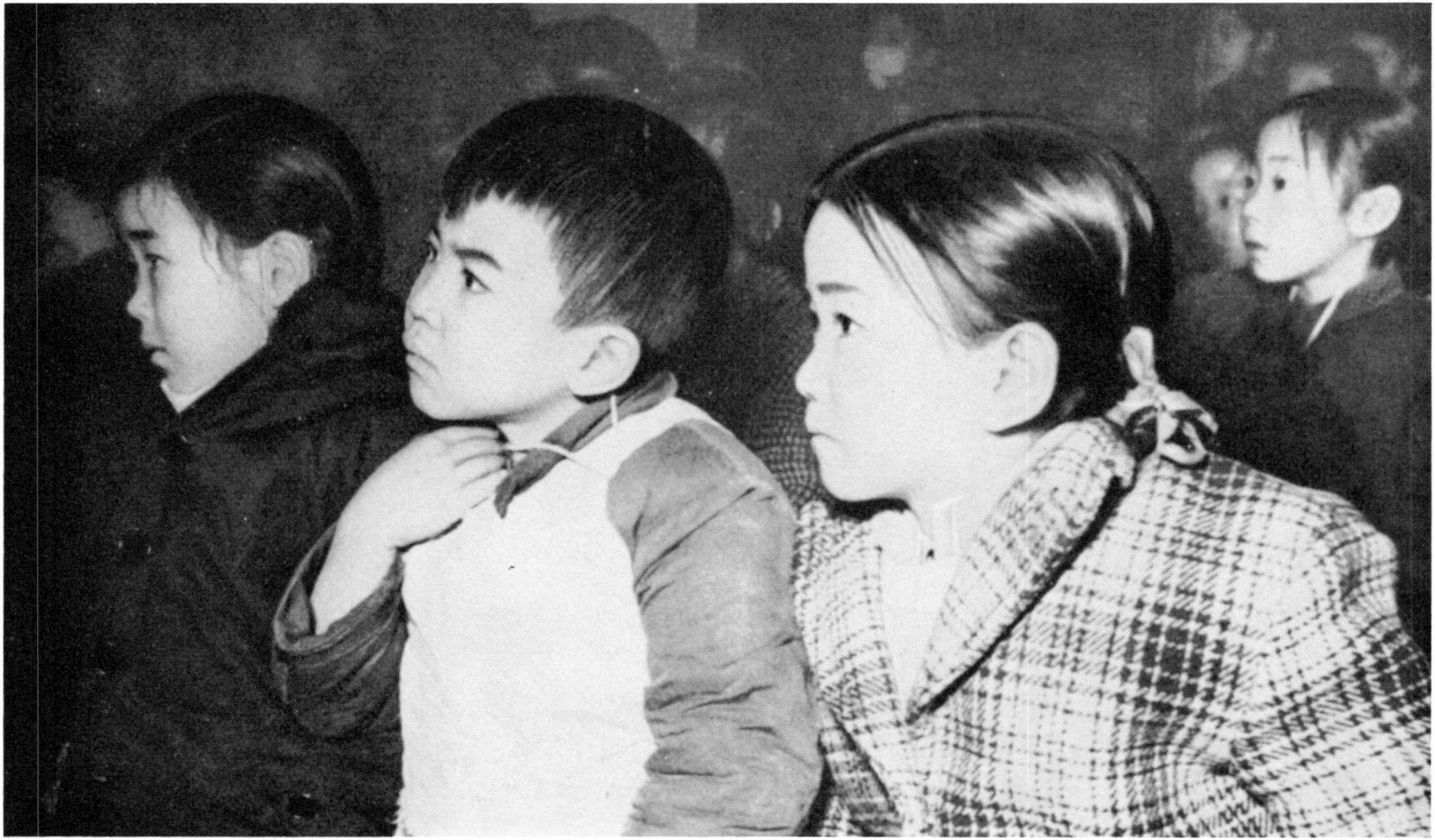

16. Spectators.

17. Shadow figures: people, horses, a tiger, and a cloud.

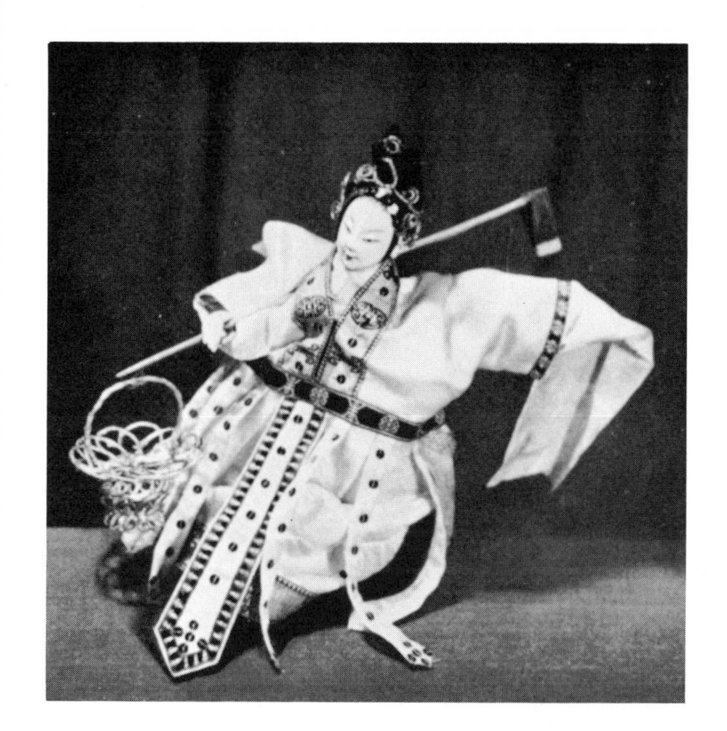

18. *The Heavenly Fairy Scattering Flowers.* Puppet theatre from the town of Tsuanchu (Fukien province).

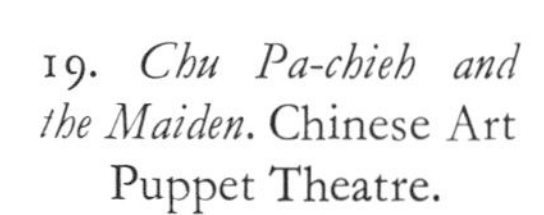

19. *Chu Pa-chieh and the Maiden.* Chinese Art Puppet Theatre.

20. Eighty-four-years' old People's Puppet Master Tsien Tsia-chu at work.

21. Puppet heads, carved by People's Master Tsien Tsia-chu.

22. Only after many years of practice can a puppeteer perform this sword dance.

23. Artists of the Tsuanchu puppet theatre (Fukien province) manipulating string puppets.

24. *The Flooding of the Monastery of the Golden Mountain.* Shadow theatre from the province of Heilungkiang.

25. Sung Wu-k'un and Chu Pa-chieh. Shadow theatre from the province of Shendui.

26. *Shao Yu-lien Saves Her Husband.* Shadow theatre from Hopei province.

27. *Burning Puyang.* Szechuan puppet theatre.

28. *The Mountain of Fiery Tongues.* Szechuan puppet theatre.

29. *The Tang Monk.* (Yuan Tsien receiving students.) Huandun puppet theatre.

30. Scene from the play *The Flour Jar*. Hunan puppet theatre.

31. *Dear Little Duckling* (*The Gosling*). Chinese Art Puppet Theatre.

32. *The Crane and the Tortoise.* Hunan shadow theatre.

33. *The Two Friends.* Hunan shadow theatre.

34. *The Builder Fox*. Chinese Art Puppet Theatre.

35. *Meeting in a Hotel*. Shadow theatre.

36. Chekhov's, *The Chameleon* as presented by the Chinese Art Puppet Theatre.

37. Young puppeteers. Chinese Art Puppet Theatre.